Enough

Also by Kris Bigalk

Repeat the Flesh in Numbers (NYQ Books, 2012)

Enough

Poems by

Kris Bigalk

NYQ Books™

The New York Quarterly Foundation, Inc.
Beacon, New York

NYQ Books™ is an imprint of The New York Quarterly Foundation, Inc.

The New York Quarterly Foundation, Inc.
P. O. Box 470
Beacon, NY 12508

www.nyq.org

First Edition

Set in New Baskerville

Layout and Design by Raymond P. Hammond

Front Cover Photo by Elizabeth Barnwell

Author Photograph by Elizabeth Barnwell

Library of Congress Control Number: 2019947952

ISBN: 978-1-63045-062-5

Enough

CONTENTS

1.

2.

3.

4.

ACKNOWLEDGMENTS

"Two Seconds" appeared in *The Good Men Project* and *Pentimento*

"On Minnehaha Creek" appeared in the anthology *Under Purple Skies*

"Miscarriage" appeared in the anthology *Open to Interpretation: Water's Edge*

"Enough" appeared in *Water~Stone Review* and *The Martin Lake Poetry Review*

"Doors" appeared in *The Good Men Project*

"Everything I say is a lie" appeared in *Identity Theory*

"Reflections on a Marriage" appeared in *Paper Nautilus*

"Stones and Stars" appeared in *The Good Men Project*

"Crow Pose" appeared in *The Martin Lake Poetry Review*

A version of "Wolf Moon" appeared in the anthology *The Night's Magician: Poems About the Moon*

"Missing" appeared in *Modern Poetry Quarterly*

"The Speed of Light" appeared in *It Starts with Hope* and *The Quotable*

"This morning, the park" appeared in *Modern Poetry Quarterly*

"A Dissection of Faith" appeared in the anthology *Open to Interpretation: Water's Edge*

"My Narcissus" (2) appeared in *here/there: poetry* and *The Good Men Project*

"After Two Months" appeared in *The Pine Hills Review*

"Notes from After" appeared in *Poetry City, USA*

"Dawn, Thanksgiving Day" appeared in *The Foundling Review*

1.

What Your Hands Held Before They Held Me

Dark coffee and cigarettes, settling the shaking, flavoring your skin,
your gun, long as a woman's leg, its contours heavy against your arm,
your dog tags, grasped in your fist, pulled tight against your neck,
a trigger, pushing against your index finger, burned by the sand,
a brother, bleeding, your hands tying the tourniquet, pressing,
another, gasping, your hands slung under his shoulders,
your ears, as the grenade detonates above your heads,
your shoulder, turned to hamburger, oozing and swelling,
your ears again, they've exploded into deafening ringing,
your mouth, to feel it moving, your neck to feel your breath,
your blood, their blood, darkening your shirt, melting into the sand.
The medic, who unclasps you from the dying soldier,
your eyes, salted, blurred, and dark with dirt,
your canteen, washing the rusty damp grit from your hands.

Slow Dancing

His skin, scented with
salt and lime, connects
to mine with a thin film of
sweat, like a bubble stuck
to a window. His fingers
taste of coffee beans and
cigarettes. His words
melt from his tongue to
my ear like drops of orange
sherbet, tangy, a little too
sweet; each taste shivers
through my eardrum, winds
its way through my brain
tumbles down my spine
and waits for his lips
to stop moving, for his
tongue to light on his
bottom lip, so I can
catch it between my teeth.

Our Language

When the candles
burn down, the red
sunset sputters,
goes black, when
we leave the last
sips of wine in
the glasses, swish
it in patterns
so the dregs
shift like dark
grains of sand...

My eyes find the space
crickets can't fill,
between where
words end and
skin meets skin.
You put your forehead
to mine, your hands
on my shoulders.
Our language is made
of small words,
muscular, kinetic,
but we leave
them silent, heavy
on our tongues.
I raise my hands
to frame your face,
stubble grazing
my wrists.

Star Gazing

Every few days new stars are born, red lumps spitting out shrapnel
the size of rice grains. For almost forty years, this universe has pushed
star-seeds out to the light, tearing tiny holes, clawing out the way
they came in, but so much more slowly, that big bang turned
to small whispers, spots of blood on the sheets, or tiny brown circles
on the backs of your t-shirts, despite the bleach.

These stars are light years away, packed in a grenade in the Colombian jungle,
and the oldest, the seven sisters, white-blue, raised and blooming, shine like
the Pleiades, like the tail of a rattlesnake, like Taurus raising his horns.
You tell me you come from the stars, and at night, when the moon
shines in the window, I press on your back. *This one?* No. *Ese?*

No Words

I compose these messages to you,
equations of letters adding up to an unprovable proof,
until you pick apart each word, each double meaning, finding in my syntax
all the things I meant too much, or didn't think to think.

And your words, buttoned up and stark as winter one day,
then naked, shivering between silences the next,
but I pretend not to notice, the space between our messages
saying more about how little each of us wants to care,
but how you know just one glance
of your fingers on the back of my hand
could say so much more
than all the pretty poetry you write.

Dear one, we are traffickers of words.
We know their limitations. Abandon them,
just love me in our language of no words, love me with your eyes,
your ears, your mouth on my mouth, your hands in my hands,
make an honest woman out of me.

Lucidity

Between sleep and waking,
I thought I felt you, eyes running down my back
like fingers too shy to press very hard,
bumping down my vertebrae in shivers.

Do you remember the way we slept, my nose
tucked behind your ear, your arm shawling
my shoulder in a detached kiss? Your hair under
my cheek, so animal, yet smelling of corn silk.

This morning, you woke, two hundred miles
north, stared at a white-gray ceiling, smelled snow
in the air. And when you turned over
you noticed her face
was most peaceful when she slept,
her feet warm, pressed
in a prayer between your knees.

If I touch your back

as you sleep, in measuring,
reaching, I have changed your
location—nearer, farther,
my fingers reach until they press
against the spongy warmth, fall
along the familiar road of your
spine, each vertebra moving before
my fingertips—have I made you
with caresses, or are you made
because I reach?

Two Seconds

In the small
of my back
a door
the size of
a fingerprint

a man grazes
his fingers
against it
and I open
like a lily

he covers it
with his palm
and my breath
ignites, a caught
match.

Ravenous

I eat half a peach, wipe the juice from my chin,
sick with its sweetness.

All I can think of is the hunger of my other mouth,
how it shapes itself to fit you,

how you harden and heat, push up against my softness,
until the juice runs out the corners,

and we stay pressed into each other like the stone
knits to the peach, grasping every indentation,

every curve.

Walking With You on Granville Island

The cherry trees shed their sweet scent in the mist,
pink-edged petals stuck to our shoes like bits of colored paper.
We walked slowly, sipping black coffee.
The sun seemed caught behind a cloud curtain,
making the light seem rare, opaque.

In a shop window, a painting of two figures
in vague silhouette, an orange sun shining
between their shoulders. It reminded us
of ourselves, so we bought it, a conception,
a birth announcement with no names.
Its rough-edged strokes and eyeless figures,
the absence of expectations.

As we crossed the bridge back to the mainland,
watched the waves billow under our feet.
How good it felt to put my cold hand in your back pocket,
have it feel so warm, so perfectly in place.

On Minnehaha Creek in May

When the willows are so new
they glow golden, letting their hair down
as they bend to the rocky creek,
lower their limbs into the water
whirling in spiral ecstasy,
this is the day when each side-step second
raises another gnat from the mud,
when each sun soaked minute
sears itself into the rhododendron buds,
when each drifting hour
brings us a little closer to the sunset,
to the melting moment
when we press our bodies together,
warm against the dewfall
as night rises, the gnats settle,
and the willows instead bend towards us, listening.

What We Expect From Each Other

The forecast in the almanac includes
the number of white clouds,
the length of afternoon shadows,
when the western sky will rain.
The morning rises, shadows
bend, our bodies' shapes turned
to daddy longlegs creeping down
the gravel road ahead of us, the cricket song
fading as the grasshopper scraping begins.

In the dead still humidity,
our backs turn to sweat,
the weeds chafe our hands.
At noon, under the cottonwoods,
we wash our faces with creek water,
guzzle lemonade, find the wild raspberries
and you set one on my tongue, where it
explodes into purple sweetness
we taste together.

Our shadows lengthen and evening comes,
the horizon a smudge-gray grumble, as predicted,
our hands twined together over the bucket handle,
dust from the road coating our nostrils.

False Spring

The sky is breathing through the open window
                    in white, like a bride or a sheet on the line
caressing our naked bodies, and it's not Spring yet, just a tease
                    promise? promise? I never asked for promises
You roll over, and my fingers press hard against
                    the muscles in your back, around your shoulder blades
and you moan a little when I roll and turn
                    my knuckles against the knots in your neck
the coconut oil slicks, melts in my hands
                    soaks into your skin, and when I taste its sweetness
in the hollow of your neck, you turn, and I feel your breath on my cheek
                    floating in rivulets around my ear, like the wind
blows in the white curtains and caresses us,
                    and I wonder if this is how it is when she
is underneath you, if you moan like this, if she bites
                    her lip and sighs when she feels the breakers
surge inside of her, and I wonder if she
                    knows which way the wind is blowing today.

Heaven

A sky full of ghosts,
space deformed
by tunnels of light,
spiral gravity twisted
into orchids of collapsed stars,
centers splaying orange pistils
that feed on the water of galaxies,
breaking through the walls of heaven,
to these summer nights on the beach
with you, a telescope, the breakers
whitening the sands, inching closer
with each lap.

Love Letter

I, whose desire for you
tastes like the paper Bibles are printed on,
tissue-thin as communion wafers,
let the ink soak into my stomach,
enter my bloodstream, settle in my brain.
Within, within, the words digest
then come together in new combinations,
my tongue both taster
and translator,
hungry and sated.

Hear me be silent.
Hear the spaces between.

These unsaid words leave a taste
in your mouth, how they ring
in your ears. Wait, wait, your teeth
set together, holding in
both the ache and the flush.
Ready yourself
for the feast.

The snow floated

like coconut flakes in the air,
like a snow globe we inhabited
alone, the glass
rounding us
like a blessing.

When you forget
yourself, you are beautiful—
I wish you saw
yourself, through a window,
or an ocean in a glass.

Your eyes are green
as the sea, your lips soft
as the snow drops
that melt on contact.

2.

Nothing Floats Forever

There are a million stars in the sky, floating—
each one a word you haven't said,
folded tight, floating towards me
in a bottle. I will catch, arrange
these bottles on a shelf,
hoping someday they will order themselves
into constellations of sentences, lines.

Tonight, in your bed, you drift
in a current. If only I could
find you in this black ocean. If only
when I did, you would open your eyes, let
me see down into the depths, let me decide
if the drowning would satisfy, or if you want
to keep floating too, ready to take my hand,
no matter which direction we choose, diving
deep, or making for shore.

My Narcissus

When you stare too long into the still pool, into your own eyes, reflect
on all the imperfections—the nose, moles, wild hair—you hate the mirror
as much as you hate yourself, and yet you still stare, hoping
for a softening, to move backwards through time,
hoping that your voice still sounds as sweet to the black-eyed
susans, the roses, the lilies, the deep purple iris.

When you sing to them, the echo floats back higher, softer,
and it wounds, shaking the aspen leaves.
You inch closer to the surface,
bending to inhale the cold water that sneers back at you,
so it enters your body,
becomes the air you breathe.

What I saw when I looked in the silver pool—

a ghost made of clouds and bone.

How time and wind clutter the sky
with vapor, my new form.

All reflections shatter
into shards of sound, less words
than tones, notes, songs
I construct when no one sings.

Narcissus kneels at the pond's opposite edge.
He will not speak, so I cannot speak.
He just gazes
into his own eyes, silvered
and glittered in the water.

I slip below the surface, settle
on the pebbled pond bottom
beneath him, look into his blue
eyes, pretending he looks at me.
I slowly float just below his face,
hoping he will bend to kiss
his own lips, as if he kissed mine.

Looking Glass

The mirror's edges tarnish, the silver backing grinding to the surface
like sand, after a winter longer than most, flavored with salt.
The middle buckles a bit, like a wave frozen,
distorts the planes of your face.
Now you know yourself differently.

You can hardly remember how easy it was to appropriate yourself,
glossed, unmarred, effortless.
No head tilting or squints, just a face that looked like yours, smiling.

No one notices your wedding ring is on the wrong hand, your mole
has moved to the other cheek. Across your forehead,
you write your name backwards, using an old eye pencil.

First Wives

I've never been a first wife,
dreams carefully arranged
like twelve fine china settings on a long
oak table where candles burned down to stubs
and no guests ever arrived, smashing
a plate or a teacup every day until the floor
is strewn with tiny knives of glass, making
any escape painful, bloody, dangerous.

Before We Met

I was the wind
and heaven blew me
out of the pink edged
eastern sky, the sun
chasing me.

I wanted to be contained,
enveloped, but struggled
against every closed door
rattling its lock, cracking
its glass with gusts
and billows.

I wanted to blow
seeds into the gardens,
rain into the rivers,
snow into the slough.
I wanted you to see
my beauty and be
stunned by it, the
container, invisible,
of all that becomes
and grows into itself.

I wanted to flip the
pages of your book
to the part where you
think of me constantly.

I wanted you to taste
the coming rain on my
lips, catch the lightning
in my hair, the sparks
turning us from elements
to stones, firm and
heavy in our certitude,
our permanence.

Miscarriage

Here, in the river, the backwater,
despite lye and bleach, the blood stain
still an outline of rust,
like the map of a lake
sketching the contours of my lap.

I never could get anything quite perfect,
always the impatient cook, the roast bleeding
onto the plate, cold to the touch
in the middle.

My porcelain sink discolored
with rust circles, crusted with
scales of lime. I scrub and scrub
but the ghosts come back,
my goblets glazed
with milky soap residue,
the very bottom of the globes
stained with dried red wine,
like my uterus once filled
with salt water, now
draining dry, this dishrag, my skirt
stained with its dregs,
the taste of iron weeping
from my tongue.

Every Great Man

Behind you, absorbing your light
I stand in the pool of your shadow,
my voice inaudible, a sonic pulse,
anechoic.

I begin a catalog of lists—
times you get thirsty: before and after sleep
how many times you smiled today: six
how many bottles in the trash bin: thirteen
how many bottles in the refrigerator: two

I will complete this chart of your moods,
if I can map the landscape of your mind.
I plot, coordinate, and draw,
your slouching silhouette a benchmark.

The surveyor, the cartographer
should touch with an invisible hand.
In this translation of your features,
I will love what you love.
I will serve it to you on the rocks.

In your shadow I become
almost transparent,
made of bones,
of tones and half-tones,
an acetate overlay of your depths,
bathymetric. Underneath
I draw a cool cerulean pool
in partial relief,
shaded.

Cognac

It tasted of gasoline, ginger, and vanilla,
scorching the throat, a wide space opening
from heart to head, a balloon inflating.

I keep falling asleep and waking up
to your snores, the bottle empty,
on its side, my mouth salted,
aching for the taste of your mouth,
but when I kiss your lips,
you turn your head into the pillow.

Day One

He sits on the cool cement front steps
next to a bottle of ginger ale.
The streetlights flicker on,
catching the glitter in the concrete sidewalk.
A little girl has drawn a hopscotch
in pink chalk, and he rolls the word
around in his mouth, "hopscotch" "hopscotch"
until it catches in his throat.

His hands so empty.

The street so quiet.

The moon is shaped like a half-empty glass,
and he's out of cigarettes.

Not Waiting Up

On the dresser, a toy bird, wooden,
dips its beak forward
towards a glass of water
and seems to drink
as his tail, the counterbalance,
pulls his head upright again.
He cannot drink.
He only appears to drink.

The grandfather clock
at the foot of the stairs,
chiming into the echo chamber
of the stairwell,
bouncing in to reverberate
near the ceiling in my
room, reminding me
every fifteen minutes
my eyes are open.

Even the tiny clicks of the hands
moving across his face are audible
at night. I cover my own face
with my hands, imagine living
the rest of my life
hidden behind precise ticking,
a mechanical kind of music.

Enough

In these last weeks before everything goes blank, white,
let's soak ourselves in maple leaves the color of summer poppies
and marigolds, let them scent our skin with cinnamon must.
Let's kick puffballs and watch the spores glide in a cloud
to find a place to sleep for the winter. Let's gather fallen twigs
and branches, run our hands along the green-mossed bark.
Let's forget, just for a few weeks, we have nothing left to say
to each other, that we've unlearned our common language,
that we have no power to turn ourselves back to the green,
unbent selves we can barely remember, except in dreams,
or blurry old photos. For now, close your eyes, let the cold wind
wash over your bare head, and just hold my hand.
It will be enough.

Narcissus in Winter

After the fifth long snow, the lake solid white blue brilliance,
his reflection fogged and frosted over, his face just a shadow,
the wind razing his cheekbones, numbing his lips, his resilience
cracks. He walks the shore, shovels away the heavy snow,
takes an auger and drills three feet down, until ice de-congeals,
the dark water rises to the surface, and he sees himself, sweaty, pale.
He uses his axe to break open a pool, sits back on his heels,
oh, how I've missed you, he repeats, breath white with each exhale.
I stand under an old willow tree, twisted and ice-glazed,
regard the full moon, a round pink ghost in the blank eastern sky,
the sun, a tepid glow on the edge of the west; his gaze
inward, rigid as frozen steel, regarding his perfection, his lie.
He leans closer to his mirror image, nose almost touching the lake;
I move behind him, build a fire, and wait for the cleft to widen,
break.

3.

Echo's Valentine

During that year he turned his eyes inward and I fell apart,
he grew smaller, concentrated into one bitter burning drop
and I expanded, turned inside out, and regarded my heart
dried like meat, cracked and turning gray as it stopped.
And I thought how sad it was that he only saw his perfect skin,
the wrapper containing this real engine of love, measuring time
in the number of beats it takes for the eyes to meet, to twin
the rhythm of oneself to another, to match the meter and rhyme
so the duet can be sung. But his duet was with himself, words
unmatched to music, playing silent between his perfect ears.
As I disintegrate, I sing the phrases I imagined he heard,
wasting my last corporeal moments wallowing in tears.
I should have walked away, let him drown in his reflection;
instead, I stayed and came undone, drowned in self-deception.

Doors

My friend sends me photographs of doors each day.
Today's was cerulean, chipping, with a cast iron grate
in front of a square window at eye level. He sends
me these doors to tempt me, remind me how long
I've stood in this doorless courtyard, where fragrant
lilies and pear trees have browned and crumpled, the wind
settling cold into my bones. A somber statue sits on
a concrete bench, staring into his hands.

This door he sent is the same color as the sky in summer.
I wish he would send a photo of a door ajar, or flung open—
a door that invites me in, keeps its promises.

Metamorphosis

I must go in; the fog is rising
  — Emily Dickinson's last words

I must go in
the fog is rising
its white wet loveliness
has erased my feet
turned the hem of my dress
into a roil.

I must go in
the fog is rising
my legs are gone
I am sinking
into this cold steam.

I must go in
the fog is rising
my hands turn into
noise—a buzzing.

I must go in
the fog is rising
I press my face to
the whiteness,
like feathers—
breathe soft brightness.

I must go in
the fog is rising
into a wild night,
nowhere to moor…

I must go in—

After Eden

No flowers left in the garden,
beheaded, their pink petals
stuck, fluttering on
overturned pots, sticking
to three small drowned
blackbirds, stray frayed
feathers washed along the path,
bodies rolled under gnarled shrubs,
beaks and talons open.

How far from the tree they fell,
lives shaken loose from a bough,
into the crevice between clouds
and the half-full rain barrel,
oak slats split in half
by the white-hot bolt,
and the dark bodies
tumbling, lungs filling,
fallen, these angels.

Aubade

This ghost of you
haunts our house, thumping
in the night, cursing softly,

rattling the locks on doors, windows,
and your body fits him, mostly,
though the shoulders must hunch

to keep the sleeves from slipping,
and the mouth is more robotic,
a straight line.

The dark cloud of frown
you've become stalks past
the breakfast table, fills his thermos,

forehead furrowed, saying nothing,
slams the door, swirls into the car,
muttering under heavy breaths.

I imagine a day when I find your note,
tucked in a book you used to love,
listing the ways you ate yourself up
from the inside out,

leaving only the bones,
a grimacing skull with empty eyes.

I prefer to stare at the low, crouching sun,
a fireball rolling down the hill, burning
its image into the fog.

The crabapple tree,

still a sapling,
thrusts out handfuls of leaves
and tight pink flower buds
this seventh spring. Sap
sweet oozes from
the green joints.
Roots, in a tremble, have
grown around the stone marker,
cradling it loose.

When my fingers
caress the first clenched buds,
my body remembers
how the boy clung to me,
how he blossomed
each time he sat on my lap
in the garden afternoons,
held his ear to my heart.

Everything I say is a lie

You say we never had an apple tree
even though I remember clearly the blossoms
on the crooked branches each spring, and how I
finally was tall enough my eighth year to reach the low
bough and swing myself up into the crook next to the trunk,
the rough bark chilly and damp against my backbone, white
petals edged with pink that worked their way into the spine
of my new book, *Little House on the Prairie*, how the new leaves couldn't
hide me from your gaze out the kitchen window.

Today, while you napped in your chair,
the pressed apple blossoms
tumbled from the pages of that yellowed, musty book
when I pulled it off the shelf.

Reflections on a Marriage

I remember us spreading the layer
of sand, arranging the stones carefully,
like puzzle pieces, sweeping the cracks
with gravel. How we marveled at the
cold geometric grayness hiding
the lumpy black dirt that had invited
weeds, stuck to the soles of our shoes.

Now no one asks what is under the stones
next to the tumble of blooms, a tangle
of flower roots thrust under and between
seeking the strength to heave
or buckle the paved present,
go back to wildness.

While you nap in a lawn chair
this afternoon, I notice the moss
creeping along the widening cracks,
fuzzy green lines.

I think of the flower roots content
in the damp underground. Is this why
we cut them off at the stems and offer
them to each other, because
we fear the naked, dirt-caked center
of ourselves? Or is it because
we can't bear to rip out
their beating hearts, leaving them
instead to die softly, alone,
under the stones?

Stones and Stars

Where the rain meets water, this stone beach,
its pebbles, granite arguments that scrape the bare
soles of our feet. You threw the first stone, I the last.
The lake rolled the stones until the sharp edges
turned soft, until their colors shone through—opaque grays,
whites, blues, the occasional agate. I collected them,
my dull pearls, strung them on fish-line, wore them like teardrops.
By sunset, you were a speck on the opposite shore, casting
your line. By nightfall, the sky cleared, and you vanished.
The moon hung sideways, a crescent in the sky,
yellow-gold, so close I could see the outline of its dark side,
the one that never turns my way.
I will soar all night, galaxies spread over my head
like a trailing silver scarf. I will breathe in the sweetness
of the rain-soaked alfalfa, tuck a small stone between
cheek and gum, and taste its unyielding.

The Worm

Walking in the April rain, head down,
the worm, pink and brown,
swollen on one end, pulsing along
on the sidewalk ahead of me, blind,
drawn out of the dirt by the slick rain.
Cruising the concrete oblivious,
looking for a hole, some tender sludgy mudslut
to eat his way into, until he is completely
swallowed up and swallowing in.

Being blind, he cannot find that slippery tunnel
of soft sweet earth, instead crawling along the cold cement,
the little beggar, soldiering along, his comrades drowning
in puddles, squashed unnoticed underfoot. I consider
how he would feel in my hand, a cool curl of flesh
with five divided hearts, a segmented love
that if cut in pieces, could survive,
even multiply.

Low Tide

The conch shell and its pink lips
hard against my teeth, its soft
animal core long eaten away,
rotted out on the beach.

Sometimes my body can't live
in the now, the now without you.
I put my finger into the hollows,
feel the cool swirl, the empty space.

Tomorrow, the tide will return, recede,
and the shells will litter the beach
like so many broken hearts—
some of them still breathing.

Missing

Long gone belonging, a silver earring, loop
hooked around itself, fashioned after its twin,
or maybe before—longing so long it curved
to meet itself so the longing would stop, or be
infinite, dispersed throughout itself like blood
inside the fascia of a wire, electricity feeding
itself instead of sparking at either end.

To miss is to long too long, unbent, uncurving,
to miss is to follow the road and not stop
to consider the ocean, the dome of the sky.
To miss is to lose oneself, like a waterfall
forgets how to fall in the winter, silvered
into a mimicry of itself, a frozen forgetfulness.

Crow Pose

After balance is lost, the limbs tumble, push into the floor,
the solid flatness cold against the rounded muscles of calf,
of forearm. Crow, how do you tip into the perfection of strength
and humor, dipping your beak to the water, then lifting your throat
so it washes down into you, turning your body to black rivulets,
feathers catching the sunlight black and blue?

Turn over the glitter of coins, the foil
of thoughts unresolvable. Let me balance on my three pronged
foot, Crow. Let me learn to fly while facing down the earth.

The First Day I Un-Loved You

I sat naked on the couch and put my feet up on the ottoman. I ate Doritos
and let the crumbs fall between the cushions, scatter on the carpet.

I did not check my phone for hours. I turned off the notifications, lay
it face down on the table, a punishment, tied and gagged.

I turned on the television and watched couples argue in front
of sarcastic judges. I watched unattractive people win cars.
I watched detectives find the truth. I watched the bad guys die.

I put all of the cheap florist vases in the recycling bin, threw out
the stale chocolates, emptied the bottle of Chanel down the sink.

I took a long, hot shower, didn't shave my legs, or wax my bikini line.
In the steam of the mirror, I saw myself as you saw me: a blurry
outline of curves in a cloud, a flesh-colored silence.

I did not wear my purple sweater dress, the one that slides across
my chest, hugs my hips, drapes down just above my knees, where
you liked to set your hand, so your thumb rested on my kneecap.

Questions are Like Keys

I can't find the right one,
but when I sit on the floor next to the spare room,
press my ear to the door,
I can hear your breathing
on the other side.

The phone keeps ringing, but you don't pick up.
Are you looking out the window at the tree with the tire swing?
Are you thinking about fixing the blind that fell down last week?
Is the intrusion of light still too much to bear?

The ghost of the man who built this house
is pacing the hallway tonight.
He pats one hand on his chest,
stumbles heavily, stares through me.
Even he, who can walk through doors, cannot
bring himself to join you.

Some of the pink and orange light spills
through the window, seeps through the cracks
between jamb and floor.

I could search for another key in the junk drawer,
or get a screwdriver and dismantle the hinges,
the lock.

But I walk out the front door, leave it wide open.
I keep walking, feel the wind gust, lift me towards the west,
where the sun, a yellow-orange yolk, paints the fields and trees.

No More Wondering

Outside, it's as if the tulips had opened their lips wide and spoken,
petals grazing her fingertips with their songs,

vibrating, almost glowing in the yellow afternoon light
asking for an echo to locate themselves.

The path through the garden, lined with black-eyed susans,
sun glinting on the birdbath, shining through the red hummingbird feeder,

sugar-sweet, syrupy, to the point of distaste.
Believing finally that the use of belief is limited,

she uses memories as spades, digging up skeletons
that used to be covered with velvet skin, smooth muscle.

To choose to be lonely is to chew on the bone, the gristle,
until there is no marrow to slither around on the tongue.

Wolf Moon

His deep, honeyed,
almost-
prayers echoed
in my ears on
good mornings, his voice
and the newborn
summer filled my
eyes, saturated
my ears like
sunlight.

His words lassoed
the edges of the Rose
Moon, his silver kisses
tasted of salt
and beer as we
rocked, his boat a cradle
underneath the canopy of pines.

Now all of that
a whisper
chilled silent evenings
spent miles apart.
He doesn't
speak, just
a photo of the scarlet
moon, *wish you*
were here
texted in the voice
of the man
who used
to tell me I
was beautiful.

4.

If it wasn't for the child

I could not have reconstructed
myself. Her hands grew
thin and graceful, and I recognized
my hands twirling her hair around
an index finger—the hair, gold and fine,
my hair, now hers, now ours, together.

A child is a resurrection of parts,
a Frankenstein's monster of best parts,
discarded parts, forgotten parts, reinvented parts,
sewn together, inseparable, into this new being.

I could not take back what I had given
without destroying her, so I held her hands,
brushed her hair, sang the songs she loved,
and at night, as she slept, I walked the meadow,
searching for the remnants of myself
only visible in the moonlight.

Where the Light Shines Through

I find pieces of myself in poems written before I was born,
about fat gold watches and nude arms waving, about Jennifer's
tigers and Blake's tyger, about bending with the remover
to remove.

I find pieces of myself on the bathroom floor, skin and fingernail
shavings, hair, each tiny fragment rife with my DNA,
that microscopic cypher, blueprint of all my imperfections.

I find pieces of myself in the back of the closet, clothes
that used to fit every curve, so I felt beautiful, so I shone.

Putting the puzzle together can be so difficult,
the picture shifting, the pieces static. Some days,
I almost finish, and when I look in the mirror,
I try not to notice the blank places,
where the light shines through.

When the mirror stops reflecting,

when everything you give falls into a hole
and you never hear it hit bottom,
when the sun stops shining and the clouds
keep gathering and blackening,
that is alone, that is lonely, that
is when you know the winter
will end, when you will burst
out of this seed-shell that holds
you, when you sit in the dark,
wishing for that moment
to come just a little faster,
and with every wish, it does.

The Speed of Light

1.
In Trondheim, the light spoke,
the light lined the streets like white
fox fur, the light soaked through the red
stained glass into the caverned cathedral,
as it had for a thousand years. Light fingered
the edges of evening as if hemming a nightgown,
never quite letting go, light cast itself against
my body to cast a long shadow against the gray
stone buildings, light pried open the roses,
light circled me like an impatient dog, whether
I ran or stood still.

2.
In Uppsala, the light was silent,
the light dusted the stones gold
in Linnaeus' garden, settled itself
at his grassy table. Light chased
the red and blue bocce balls strewn
on the court, turning the grass translucent.
Over a hollow willow tree, the light
coaxed out green branches from the
apparently dead wood, and led their
delicate leaves down into the pond,
a veil of shadows, an artifact
of thought only visible
when I stood still, only palpable
when I walked through it.

Origami: Lines for Joe

Once you hold
a belief, it folds
itself into a flower,
an ear, a star.

In your deepest dreams,
it rises, unfolds itself,
as if inflated
by a breath,
blooming.

When you wake,
the creases stay, wish
for the edges of the shape
they once made.

Sunrise in Winter

Horizon's door
by which the mammatus
clouds wait, breasts letting
down their milk in a spill
of white drops,
flakes like white seeds,
a rain come too late; the cold sun
burns wan and white as it
spreads bright wings of violet,
orange, and pink overhead,
an unfurling canopy.
The snow in a grand glitter,
its sun-sparks flame out
like shining shards of sunrise
dew that shook from
the edges of the sunflower
now brown, heavily foiled
with a white blur, bleared
against the gray-brown
dappled stones.

This morning, the park

full of trilling bright bluebirds
empty of people;
cerulean brushstrokes flit
from tree to tree, sixteenth-notes
blooming on a staff
of a dewy cast iron fence;
silence like a gate
ajar, waiting for warm wind
to blow open shade to day.

A Dissection of Faith

One half relies on the details
of photosynthesis
a religion of chlorophyll and light—

the other half is
held up by oceans.

A leaf, a stepping stone, leading flesh
to air, focusing the mind's eye.
See, an entrance to a tree knot,
the scent of sweet sap
circling like a catacomb.

My Narcissus

My narcissus was a gift, a raw round heart encased in paper-brown skin that flaked off in my hands. He slept in my palm, nestled into the dark space as my thumb closed around him.

After I put him into his bed, covered with cold earth, I waited, and he opened his fist, reached up through the soil with his three fingered hand.

You know the rest of the story, how he became lost in himself, drowned in his idea of himself.

All that's left now is his withered body, cut off, turning to dirt, the snow slowly burying him. But his heart, the one I loved first, beats underground.

What I Didn't Hate About You

The way your eyes warmed golden when you smiled,
how it felt to run my fingers through your hair,
and how your hands skimmed along my hip, my waist,
my breast, how your cheek felt after you shaved
in the morning, how it felt when you pressed it
rough against my neck. The way you said good morning,
the way you said good night, the way you cried
the last time you shut the door.

After Two Months

in a burned-black room
the curtains blowing
the scents of autumn's end—
caramel smoke, with an edge
of chill, of rain, of endings,
and then
sweet softness
your gentle bearded cheek
sliding alongside my body
until your mustache
rested on my upper lip
and the cool mint
of your tongue slid
to meet mine.
I woke, but didn't open
my eyes.

I know that ephemera
only rides the wind
and doesn't circle back.

I know the way mist
gives way to rain,
then to snow.

So I waited, eyes closed,
and listened to the curtains
whisper, smelled the last
of the bonfire embers,
held my hand
to my cheek,
where your breath
left its warmth.

When I Had Time

It snowed the day down in fat flakes
somewhere between zero and thirty degrees.
My fingers rambled the piano, the window
letting in some weak blue light, my eyes
catching the tumbling flakes as they made
large figure eights, some lighting on the window
and melting, as aimless and short-lived as my tune.

When I had time for missing you,
I dreamed I found your footprints
in the snow and tried to follow them, setting
my bootsoles into your footprints,
so we made one path.

I imagined I'd become you, but I didn't.
And when I lost your trail, deep in the woods,
I began my own, in your memory, following
the tree line back to the house
as night melted in, just like always.

Notes From After

A hole in the ice, jagged as a smile made with sawteeth.
You, gone, slipping underwater through the frozen air.

The sky unrolls itself so I can spell your name with star points.
I can never quite remember where I started.

This sleep, heavy, stuffed with feathers, warm, unfamiliar, close.
I carry it into midnight like a sleeping baby, cradled.

Singular

I wonder if I've ever been on the right side of love.
Love always seemed so quick, so difficult to catch,
like a dragonfly, amber and glowing on a sunflower,
gone the second I try to clasp my hands around him.
I let love go free and he never returned, which according
to bad greeting cards means he was never mine to begin with,
that he never saw me as an attractive jailer or keeper.
I never really wanted a beautiful prisoner anyway.
If love could alight on my shoulder in this sunset, translucent
wings catching pink and gold, tiny legs perching on my skin,
that might be the closest I come to speaking with God in this life.

Dawn, Thanksgiving Day

Clouds cover most of the stars,
though Libra straddles the half-moon
behind a gray-wisp curtain, and Scorpio
grasps at the gibbous with his claws,
the creep of atmosphere gradual as
a thickening cataract, until the blindness
seems like it's always been there, a speck
that grows to a spot, slowly collects
into a frost pattern, edging
the window-glass like a frame.

The clouds pink, then blanch—
snow soon, its breath invisible, a heavy
clean scent. One chickadee at the feeder,
trees deserted of leaves, save for a sloppy
squirrel nest. This, my one hour of silence,
this window-staring flight from a coffee-
stained to-do list. We stay where we
survive, don't we, where the landscape claims
us, where the rest of our kind wait
for us, perched on treetops or
on wires, singing a tune
we've known all our lives.

My Narcissus

The rag I use to clean the floor is flannel, green plaid,
a scrap of the shirt I bought for you ten years ago,
that you wore every weekend, soft and warm, clad
for the sharp fall afternoons raking leaves, windblown,
the winter nights by the fireplace, keeping us warm,
the spring planting of apple trees, willows, and bulbs,
the summer nights tending the firepit, watching the morning
star rise in an arc. That shirt held the sweet smell of smoke,
and even now, as I scrub, the scent of charcoal, burnt, rises
out of the soapy rag, and I wonder if you ever think
about the parts of you that got lost, if what you prize
has changed since we last spoke. Whether scent or stink,
the cloth sticks to my thoughts, reminds me of the old you,
whose lonely offices brought me joy, who never knew.

CPSIA information can be obtained
at www.ICGtesting.com
Printed in the USA
FFHW020827051119
55952454-61785FF